Holding On While Letting Go:
A Director's Guide to Contemporary Talent Management

OTHER TITLES:

Woodruffe, C. (1999). *Winning the talent war: A strategic approach to attracting, developing and retaining the best people.* **Chichester: John Wiley**

Woodruffe, C. (2007). *Development and assessment centres: Identifying and developing competence, 4th edition.* **London: Human Assets Ltd.**

Human Assets Limited
3 Clifford Street
London W1S 2LF
tel: +44 (0)20 7434 2122
fax: +44 (0)20 7434 1905
web: www.humanassets.co.uk

HOLDING ON WHILE LETTING GO:

A Director's Guide
to Contemporary
Talent Management

Charles Woodruffe • **Wendy Lyons** • **Jasmin Silver**

Human Assets Limited

Published by Human Assets Ltd. All rights reserved. No part of this publication
may be reproduced, stored in an information storage and retrieval system, or
transmitted in any form or by any means, electronic, mechanical, photocopying,
recording or otherwise, without the written permission of Human Assets Ltd,
3 Clifford Street, London W1S 2LF

Design by **Laura Hunter Designs**

Printed by **Lightning Source**

ISBN 978–0–9554488–1–2

CONTENTS

Our aim in writing this book is to help you tackle the tricky contemporary issues in talent management. Quite obviously, the backdrop for talent management has been transformed with the changing fortunes of the economy. For plenty of organisations 'letting people go' is forced upon them to balance the books. Yet, organisations will only come through these difficult times by dint of the people working in them.

We hope that you find our treatment of the issues helpful. We would very much welcome your feedback and the chance of discussion with you. We can be contacted at charles.woodruffe@humanassets.co.uk

We summarise the latest research on talent management on our website www.humanassets.co.uk and invite you to sign up for our monthly e-newsletter by visiting the site.

We are grateful to our colleagues and clients who have contributed to the thinking represented in this book. We are also very grateful to Laura Hunter who got our material ready for publication.

Charles Woodruffe
Wendy Lyons
Jasmin Silver

London, February 2009.

THE WAR FOR TALENT

IN TOUGH ECONOMIC TIMES, ORGANISATIONS MUST CUT STAFF COSTS TO SURVIVE BUT ALSO BE OBSESSED WITH RETAINING PEOPLE

t might be a cliché but it is also the truth: Whether we are in a boom or bust, talented people are the key to your organisation's success. This is a truism to every business leader who knows that most businesses compete through the quality of their people. It is their people that give them the edge with their customers – both directly in customer-facing roles and indirectly through innovation and leadership. What is more, this truth applies as much in the public and not-for-profit sectors as in the private sector. If a school or hospital is not to be a 'failing' organisation, it needs good people.

Although having good people has always been important, what has undoubtedly changed in the last twenty years is the level of competition faced by organisations. What has also changed is the clarity of the simple truth that, in any sector, people are at the root of your competitive edge. In some sectors, this might be a few exceptional people who come up with ingenious products or business ideas; in many sectors the competitive edge is gained by the mass of employees who have direct or indirect dealings with customers. An advantage over competitors is achieved by a mix of innovative products, approaches or solutions, designed by a few people, and product delivery that is the responsibility of many people. All in all, as illustrated in Figure 1, a key element of the business strategy is a people strategy – you compete by having the best people. If anything, this is even more true in a recession. In many sectors only the best organisations – basically, those with the best people – will survive in the competition for a diminished customer spend.

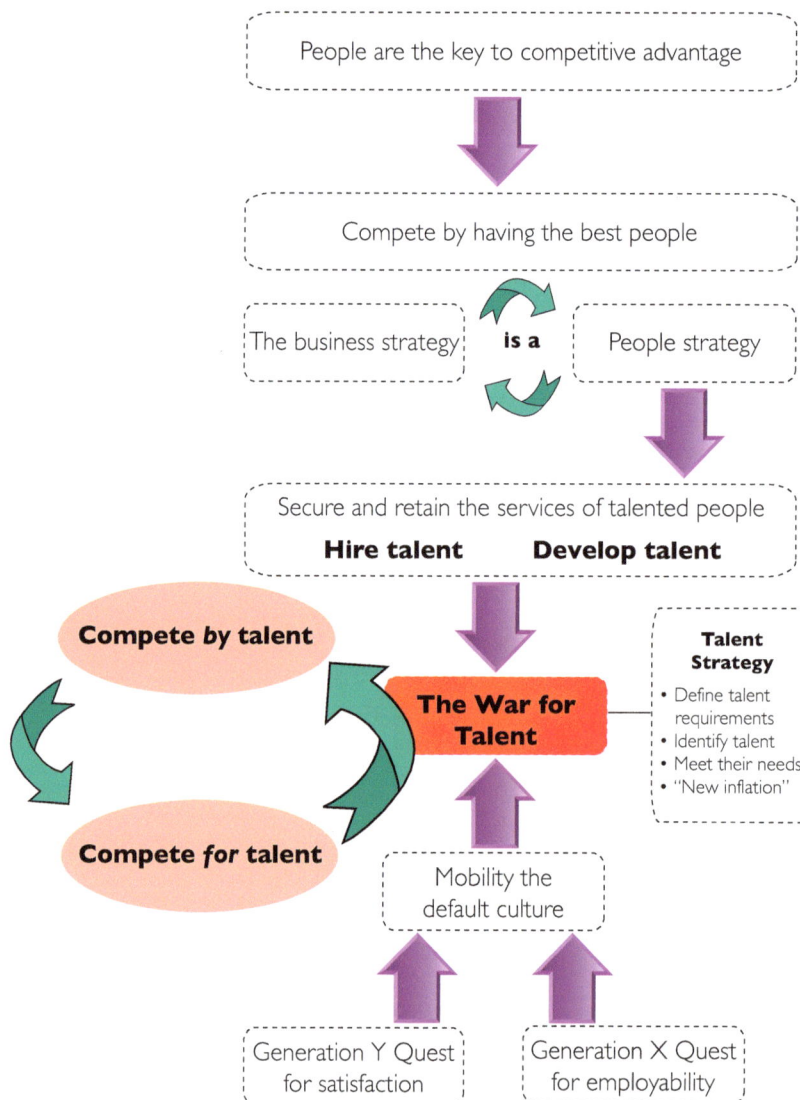

Figure 1. The War for Talent

As customers of both private and public sector organisations, we have all become far more demanding – and now, as consumers, also more reluctant – than we were a generation ago and moving our custom has become as easy as the click of a mouse. Think what we put up with just twenty years ago. Shops were shut more than they were open; airlines charged the earth for weekday travel; hospitals had enormous waiting lists; 'jobs-worth' characters were commonplace in everything from deliveries to the local council. We might have grumbled, but we also suffered. Nowadays we have both choice and impatience with second best. In some sectors, particularly public services, we demand that staff are at least 'good enough'. In many sectors, we migrate our custom to whoever provides the very best in terms of product and service. Why go to a good enough solicitor if you can afford the best? Why fly with a good enough airline if the best will take you to the same destination for a similar price?

At precisely the same time that organisations are trying to employ the best people to steal a march over each other, these prized assets have themselves become more fickle. The norm of careers has changed to one of mobility. Furthermore the best people know perfectly well that they are sought after. Before the recession, headhunters would call routinely to remind them of this fact and even nowadays many organisations are still looking to assess the availability of the best people at their rivals. What is more, organisations have wetted the appetites of staff by trying to satisfy hitherto unknown needs. Organisations offer everything from flexible work to cafeteria benefits. The moment one employer offers a new feature to attract and retain people, every member of staff puts it on their wish list. Nowadays, having perfect credentials in corporate social responsibility has become an entry level condition for the employers of Generation Y, having been an unknown concept only a decade ago.

So was born the war for talent. Organisations need talented people to win but talented people are never truly won – they have to be re-engaged every day. Furthermore, although there are some sectors where people, like their products or services, just have to be 'good enough', there are many other sectors where good enough is not enough. You have to have the best if you are to win, be it the best designers, the best professionals or the best at customer service. Securing and keeping the best people is an inexorable challenge.

We have, then, two competitions. One is for customers – a competition that is won *by* talented people. The other is the competition *for* talented people. Undoubtedly the increased emphasis on competing by talent has added momentum to competing for talent. Equally though, competing for talent has focused organisations on the fact that they compete by talent. And that concentration adds renewed vigour to the competition for talent.

So we have it that talent has come to the forefront of the agenda for the human resources function. Many sizeable organisations have a talent manager and a talent strategy and consultancies abound to offer to help firms with their task of winning the war for talent. The number of conferences and books on talent has mushroomed and the Chartered Institute of Personnel and Development (CIPD) provide a talent management toolkit (Cannon & McGee, 2007).

The objective of talent management is ensuring the organisation has the people resources it needs to fulfil its business strategy. As an objective, it can be traced back to succession planning and manpower planning aimed at identifying the talent pipeline. But the process and backdrop are different. Talent management acknowledges that people are transient and places much more emphasis than its forebears on retaining people. It used to be almost assumed that all the organisation had to do was identify the right people and develop them and then they would be there when the time came. Now identifying people is just the start. The key is to ensure you keep them.

A proper talent management system sets up a virtuous circle. Not only does the systematic identification and development of talent enable the organisation to provide for its future requirements. It also acts as a beacon to employees of the possibilities that are open to them, thereby encouraging retention. In short, appointing employees already working for your organisation to vacant positions serves many purposes such as reducing costs per hire, reducing initiation time as the employee is already familiar with the organisation and its culture and improving retention by giving employees development in terms of career progression.

All this is just as true in bad times as well as good. Indeed, arguably, organisations will depend even more on the best people to survive when they have their backs against the economic wall. In these circumstances, when cost cutting might require redundancies, talent management is not essentially changed. The key issue becomes making cuts in a way that does not lose the most critical talent. In order to do this, organisations require a carefully devised talent management strategy firmly rooted in business reality and focussing on assessing people in each talent pool – being incisive on what you want from people and clearly determining those who demonstrate these behaviours and who will be priorities for the development budget and retention efforts.

A recent survey that Human Assets carried out showed that the recession has also introduced its own considerations in the war for talent. Of course, people are less able to leave but employers are very concerned that the best people will also be less easy to attract. A star in one organisation is going to be far more wary of moving in a recession than in a boom. What if it does not work out?

What if the new employer has to retrench? In this new era, employers have to work even harder to gain the trust of people to join them. In some sectors such as finance with very tarnished reputations this will require a lot of effort.

Furthermore, the recession is increasing the need for the skilful engagement of people. While employers can, quite rightly, demand that everyone pulls together to survive, it is also clearly not enough to motivate people simply to remind them they are lucky to have a job. If cuts have been made either by redundancies or in people's development and expectations, employers have to work extra hard to keep people engaged and not storing resentments that will be exercised when better times return.

We have it then that the recession has introduced the particular difficulty of making necessary cuts while not tarnishing carefully constructed reputations and trust. More than ever, all the components of talent management must be aligned in an overall strategy. Any incoherence and contradiction in talent management will be rapidly spotted. Talent management covers the full requirement that organisations must attract, choose, develop and retain the best people if they are to be winners. It is about all these matters that this guide is concerned. But, at the outset, 'talent' must be defined.

CHAPTER ONE

DEFINING TALENT

THOUGH THEY COMPETE FOR TALENT AND WITH TALENT, EACH ORGANISATION STRIVES TO DEFINE TALENT DIFFERENTLY

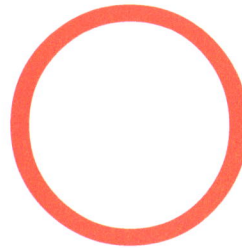

Organisations have to attend to their talent in two senses of the word. Firstly, they need to stock and have successors to their élite. Secondly, they need to make sure that all their staff are competitive with and preferably better than their rivals.

TALENT AS ÉLITES

Every organisation must provide both for those who occupy, and those who are best suited to succeed to, leadership positions. The élite groups might also include other staff who are difficult to replace, such as people with a particular technical or professional expertise.

In dealing with élites, talent managers must ensure that the slots for such people are identified and kept filled. The organisation needs a future CEO as well as, say, the expert on Bermudan taxation or the cardiothoracic surgeon.

TALENT AS EVERYONE

The second focus for talent management is potentially everyone within the organisation. Everyone plays a part directly or indirectly in the customer experience and so everyone is part of the firm's talent. In the hospital, the friendly cleaner or porter is key to the patient's experience; in the supermarket the checkout staff can make all the difference for shoppers. In this sense, talent management is much of the firm's human resources management.

TALENT POOLS

Given the range that is covered by talent management, it is best to follow the practice of thinking in terms of talent pools. Roles within organisations are not homogeneous and it makes sense to focus on the people for a group of roles which make similar demands and treat them as a talent pool. Some pools will be élites such as the civil service's high potential pool or the junior partner pool at a professional services firm. Other pools will be composed of the serried ranks of mainstream staff.

The key activity of the talent manager is to ensure that each talent pool is stocked with people of the required calibre through attracting, choosing, developing and retaining them. But before that, the manager must specify what qualities people need if they are to be included in a talent pool. In other words, what are the talents that talented people must possess to be counted as 'the talent'?

INDICATORS OF TALENT

Our own approach at Human Assets has been to pioneer and advocate Indicators of Excellence. These specify in a straightforward way what it is that a person needs to do excellently if they are to make the maximum strategic contribution in their role. What does the bank teller have to do excellently? What does the finance director have to do excellently? What does the housing officer have to do excellently? We can ask the same questions of people in pools of potential. What does the person in the 'emerging talent' pool of potential future executives have to do now in order to remain in the pool? We only know someone has potential because something they do distinguishes them from others. What is it? As illustrated in Figure 2, we start with the organisation's strategy and then pinpoint the role's contribution to the strategy. We then move directly to what people have to do excellently in their roles or talent pools. This covers both what they must do in the sense of achievements (e.g., problem solving; customer satisfaction) and in terms of an approach (integrity; team collaboration) that is key to the organisation.

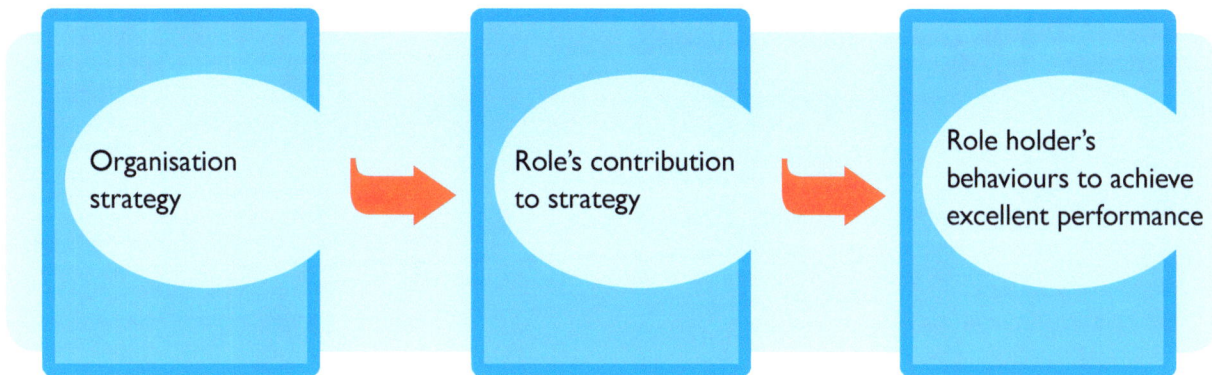

Figure 2. From strategy to excellence

The indicators of excellence approach results in far pithier lists than the typical competency framework.

Some examples are provided in the tables below.

HIGH POTENTIAL JUNIOR LEADER

Contribution of role to XXX's strategy

Makes an immediate contribution to own part of the business and strives to develop for senior leadership roles

Indicators of excellence

- Works with independence and consistently completes assignments on time and to required standard
- Confident and deft in dealing with seniors, peers and juniors
- Takes advantage of, and puts self forward for, developmental opportunities
- Incorporates strategic business context into work
- Analyses and thinks way through complex /novel problems
- Remains objective, calm and emotionally neutral in testing situations
- Advances well thought-out views based on logic and political realities
- Maintains a positive 'can do' approach to change
- Considers the status quo and makes reasoned recommendations for improvements

MERGERS & ACQUISITIONS TEAM LEADER

Contributor of role to XXX's strategy

Top quality transaction work delivered to clients – 'From work won by directors to work done by teams'

Indicators of excellence

- Thorough understanding of all aspects of the transaction – its strategic business case, the parties to the transaction, the regulatory climate and the 'project plan'
- Ensures delivery of requirements are error-free and to time
- Comes up with creative proposals to progress the transaction and actions these or conveys to director as appropriate
- Motivates and develops all members of transaction team ensuring their talent is properly used and managed and that workloads are achievable
- Is seen as thoroughly credible by and liaises with all external parties – client (FD and CEO) and lawyers
- Maintains active communication with transaction director
- Develops professional knowledge base and network to become seen as expert in their transaction area

QC ADVOCATE

Contribution of role to XXX's strategy

Provides clients with legal advice on matters of complexity and advocates their case

Indicators of excellence

- Gains a rapid, incisive overview of complex and voluminous material
- Identifies the course of action that will produce the best outcome for the client, giving priority to non–court resolution throughout the case where appropriate
- Is up to date with law and precedent relevant to each case dealt with, or will quickly and reliably make self familiar with new areas of law
- Appreciates aspects of the case that are particularly important, sensitive or difficult
- Identifies the best arguments to pursue and anticipates points that will challenge an argument
- Rapidly assimilates implications of new evidence and argument for own case and responds appropriately
- Communicates the case in a persuasive manner to achieve the best outcome for the client
- Provides effective leadership to the client and the advocate team
- Demonstrates unwavering integrity, being honest and straightforward in professional dealings with all parties

Table 1. Three sets of indicators of excellence

CONTRAST WITH COMPETENCIES

Competencies are elicited by asking what behaviours a successful person exhibits in comparison to a less successful performer. In deriving a competency matrix, the behaviours are clustered with the aim of producing a model of the person who will be a high performer – essentially, a model of the traits that they will exhibit. This leads to a relatively large number of competencies because the researcher is trying to avoid combining traits that are psychologically distinct.

After a promising start, competencies suffered from their inherent cumbersomeness. Though some have been jettisoned, many organisations have competency frameworks that managers find difficult or impossible to make practical use of. It is only slightly unfair to cite the NHS Knowledge and Skills Framework (Department of Health, 2004), the documentation for which extends to 267 pages weighing 1.135 kilograms. While, no doubt, this is easier to use than first appearances suggest, it is the first appearances that set the tone in managers' minds.

LIMITATIONS OF COMPETENCIES

Having worked on the Indicators of Excellence approach with the motivation to make things simpler and more manager-friendly, we started to compare them more formally with competencies and identified a number of ways in which the Indicators is a better approach.

Competencies have never been entirely accepted. There are concerns that far from encouraging diversity, they encourage cloning, that they are rooted in the past rather than the future and that they fail to incorporate the organisation's values. Each of these criticisms can be answered, to some extent at least. But lingering doubts remain: Competencies allow room for differences but the maverick might be excluded; research on competencies can ask about the future but it is rather contrived asking about the high performer of the future in comparison to the low performer; values should be embedded in the behaviour of high performers but they are not necessarily explicit.

A further and fundamental problem is that competencies involve a step back from performance to an attempt at measuring the factors (competencies) behind performance. The assumption is that the person with the factors in abundance will be a high performer. However, there are bound to be errors of both omission and commission in the list of competency behaviours and the way that they are clustered is more art than science. As a consequence, we have no guarantee that high performance will follow from possession of the competencies. Furthermore, nobody will come with all the competencies in high measure and the unanswered question is which weaknesses will destroy performance. Think analogously of trying to unpack the motor racing driver's competencies and then predicting future stars from measuring these supposed components of talent. It will only take you so far and, we believe you would have been far better off observing the overall performance of the young Lewis Hamilton in his go-kart than measuring him competency by competency.

For organisations that have simplified but not abandoned their lists of competencies, the danger is that the potential for a disconnection between competencies and performance increases as the list of competencies is pruned and simplified. We believe that, rather than trying to cluster the behaviours of high performance into pseudo-psychometric variables behind performance, we would be much better off ordering behaviours by the strategic outputs that they achieve. Of course, we could easily end up measuring 'apples and pears' together as components of a given output. There does not seem any problem with this: The sum total of the behaviours adds up to high performance.

Indicators of excellence differ from competencies, then, by being purely and simply the excellent behaviours that will make the maximum contribution to strategy. As Figure 3 suggests, the origins of these behaviours that determine whether they are in our repertoire are many and varied and will depend on the specific behaviour. Learning will probably make the biggest contribution but we should also include the motivations, preferences, abilities and values that make the display of the behaviour more likely. These are the result of the complex interaction between heredity and environment. The precise details will vary both with the person and the behaviour. In other words what has led me to be able, say, to make an excellent presentation is different to what has led you to the same behaviours.

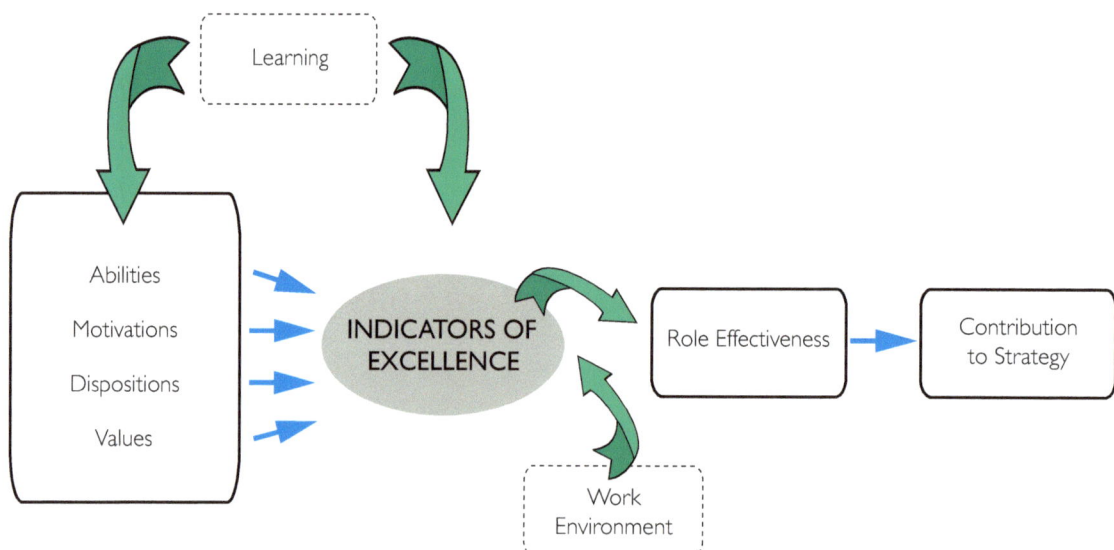

Figure 3. The hub of excellence

SUMMARY

We believe it is time for competencies to be moved forward. We need to adopt a more direct and straightforward approach to specifying the behaviours that denote high performance. High performance means achieving strategic outputs. We should specify the outputs and then identify the behaviours required for the outputs

The required behaviours will only be displayed **a)** if the person is capable of displaying them, **b)** if the person wishes to display them and **c)** if the situation encourages them to be displayed. So behaviour is a function of both the person (who must be willing and able) and the situation (which acts to encourage or discourage particular behaviours). In selection we are ensuring the organisation chooses people who already demonstrate the required behaviours or demonstrate the greatest potential to be able to do so. In development we are converting potential into performance. In engagement and retention we are ensuring that capable people join, stay with and are positive towards the organisation. In performance management we are ensuring that the organisation encourages people to display the required behaviours – that the 'press' from the environment is strong and clear to people. All these matters come together in the talent management strategy – to which the next chapter turns.

THE STRATEGIC OVERVIEW

A REPUTATION FOR TALENT MANAGEMENT BUILT OVER YEARS CAN BE DESTROYED BY ONE SMALL GAP IN CREDIBILITY.

Talent management deals with a large number of inter-related variables. Change one variable – for example how you choose people – and you change others – for example the attraction and retention of people. Furthermore, whatever you do to the immediate variables of talent management has an impact beyond the mere supply of talented people – change the employer brand and it impacts on the customer brand; your diversity policy impacts on the ability to win public sector contracts. And so on.

It is because of these inter-relationships and the huge potential for unintended consequences from acting on any one variable that talent management really does need to be based upon a well-considered strategy. How you set about ensuring an ongoing supply of talented people for your business must be thought through with care.

As discussed in the last chapter, and illustrated in Figure 4 the starting point is the design of the organisation so that it can meet its business objectives. The design will define the roles in the organisation and enable the tentative grouping of these roles into talent pools. However, at the outset, there has to be a dialogue between the business strategy that dictates the design of the organisation and the talent strategy that is designed to supply the people. Can the desired number of people with the necessary capabilities be found as required by the business strategy? If not, the business strategy, or at least the design of the organisation, must be modified. This might not sound very impressive to a demanding CEO but the talent manager has to reflect back the reality of what can be done. Maybe an aggressive growth plan needs to be tempered; maybe expansion would be better by acquisition of another firm's talent than by organic growth; maybe the organisation should be stocked by self-employed rather than full-time staff.

After this initial dialogue, the talent manager will have what is seen as a deliverable requirement. The strategy is then all about how to deliver it. With roles clustered into talent pools, the strategy must provide for the right number of people within each talent pool now and into the future. For example, the talent manager needs to provide for leadership of the organisation. This covers the immediate leadership and – perhaps more importantly – a leadership pipeline to cover future requirements.

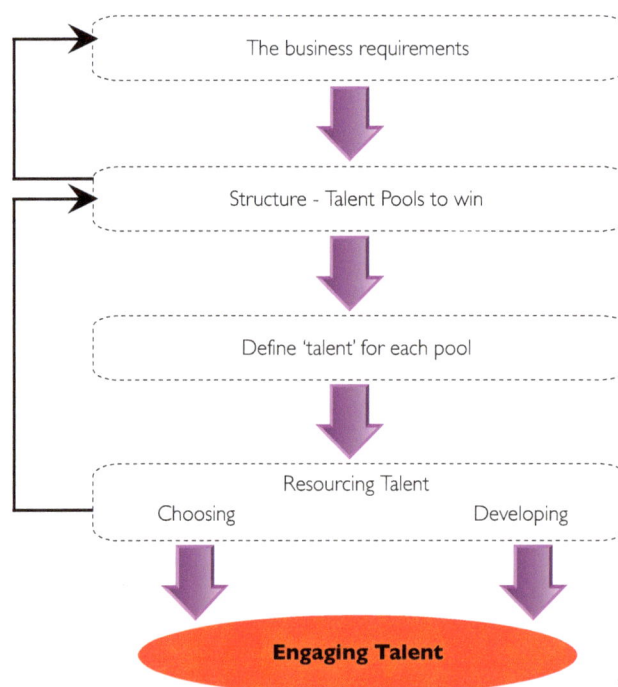

Figure 4. The flow of talent

Figure 5 below illustrates one answer to this need for a leadership pipeline. It deals with the organisation at a reasonably high level of generality but shows the identification of people for development **a)** to the executive and senior leadership positions **b)** to management roles and **c)** to team leadership.

People are chosen for development programmes to prepare them for these three levels of leadership. Then of, course the detail of how to choose and develop them needs to be tackled, alongside how to attract and engage people in these talent pools. Each of these segments of talent management is

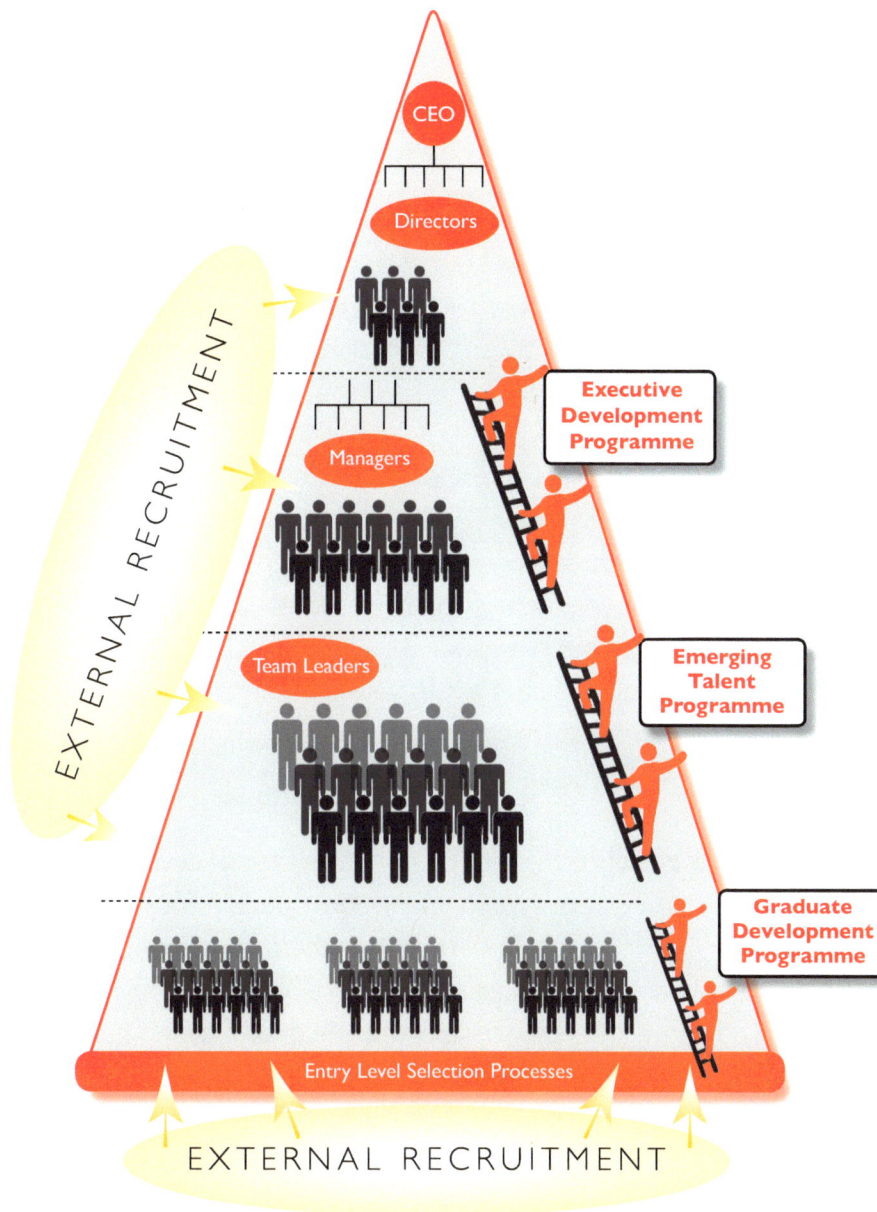

Figure 5. Ensuring a leadership pipeline

dealt with in the following chapters. However, the talent manager also needs to have an overview of these matters interacting with each other and acting together to deliver talent to the organisation.

Precisely how an organisation specifies its talent pools and the detail of its talent strategy will depend on its circumstances and requirements. The sum total of the talent management strategy will spell out how the organisation is going to have the talent it needs. It requires detail on how the organisation will attract, choose, develop and engage people and these matters are considered in the next chapters. However, there are also common questions and issues that transcend each piece of the talent management jigsaw and which must be continually re-visited when each of the elements of talent management is being addressed. Key amongst these overview questions are the following:

1   **You need to know** the numbers of people required for each talent pool and when the requirement is forecast. You also need to be able to include the knock-on effects on other talent pools of providing for succession to any particular pool. For an organisation of any size, you will need software to help you with your talent modelling in the same way that you need software for financial modelling.

2   **You need to consider** how long you can keep people waiting for promotion without losing them. If you have someone earmarked for a particular succession, what can you do to keep them interested in the interim? Nowadays, people have a relatively low tolerance of waiting in the wings. Quite apart from anything else, they have a justified suspicion that their time might not come after all, having been overtaken by events.

3   **You need to resolve** the tension between internal development plus promotion and external recruitment. Some people consider external recruitment to yield the benefit of refreshing the organisation's DNA. However, it is demotivating for people who are hoping to progress internally. They leave, thereby increasing the need for external recruitment. The precise way that the tension is resolved will depend upon such factors as the depth of internal talent and the viability of bringing in senior people from outside.

4 **You need to ensure** alignment of every element of talent management with all the other elements and with the overall employer brand. You also need alignment between the employer brand and the marketing brand. As examples, tales of bonuses paid by banks have tarnished their reputation with customers; a badly handled internal assessment process can result in disengagement; you might cut development and hope to buy people in as required but in order to attract them you must promise development.

All these questions and their interactions will need to be considered in arriving at your overall talent strategy. The end result should be a coherent and robust route-map for ensuring that you have now and into the future the people you need for your organisation to meet its business strategy.

A STRATEGY FOR DIVERSITY

Talent management sits very well with the contemporary push for organisations to have in their employment and at all levels of seniority, a profile of staff that broadly reflects the society in which the organisation operates. Talent management is essentially a diversity-embracing exercise. The objective is to identify all the talent available to the organisation, whatever might be people's ethnicity, gender, sexual orientation, age and disability etc.

Yet, despite espousing diversity and wanting talent, what many organisations still do is somewhat contrary. They want the best people for their positions but still leave the dice loaded in favour of white, reasonably privileged, able bodied men. There is still a lack of inclusiveness – the selection day is on

a religious festival for some applicants; the disabled candidate cannot easily get into the workplace; the training event runs on to an hour when the mother needs to be on her way home.

For those on the receiving end, such acts lead to a feeling of exclusion. And the problem is that many elements of talent management suffer from the repercussions. First, organisations fail to avail themselves of the best people. Second, organisations with a narrow talent base will not offer a reasonable reflection of their broader customer-base and will seem out of touch with those customers. Third, people working within organisations who feel excluded are likely to become disengaged and not give their best to their jobs. Fourth, all staff nowadays want to see corporate social responsibility (CSR) taken seriously by their employer and actions that fail to include minorities will disrupt CSR credentials.

Each of these arguments might be shrugged off – but to do so would be erroneous. The table below sets out the reasons for inclusion, the counter-arguments – the 'why bother?'

ARGUMENT	OBJECTION	COMMENT
You need the best people and therefore must include all talented people.	We have plenty of applicants of the right quality without bothering to be inclusive.	*Might* be true for low level jobs. But for top jobs you need the best people, not just 'good enough' people.
You need your people to reflect your customer base.	Our customers are not that diverse.	That's the argument! A more diverse workforce might attract more – and more diverse – customers.
If you do not include people, they will not give their best.	I won't allow them to be that disengaged.	It is a lot less effort to have staff voluntarily engaged to 'go the extra mile' than having to coerce them to perform.
All staff want to see CSR credentials and inclusion is part of that.	We are perfectly ethical and principled. If you want more, we will support a local charity.	People are extremely vigilant to hypocrisy and lack of authenticity. If you want to engage people you have to really believe your message.

objections – and it also discusses how those objections might not be such great grounds for complacency.

The truth is that we now live in an era when being inclusive and aware of the issues of diversity are simply a must for contemporary organisations. They are a must both to secure customers (particularly if the public sector is within their customer base) and to secure talented staff (particularly the contemporary Generation Y worker who is vigilant to an employer's standards).

What organisations need to do is to get a step ahead of their legal obligations and overcome the hurdles that cause groups of people to be under-represented – particularly at senior levels.

Human Assets has recently been working with one of the largest UK government departments on part of its programme to help people from under-represented groups achieve their potential. The department runs a one year development programme for a small number of carefully selected staff who have a disability or are from ethnic minorities. The programme starts with a one day development centre that helps participants consider the personal and organisational impediments to their advancement. Top amongst the personal impediments is a straightforward lack of self-belief. It is a well-researched fact that white males are the least bashful at putting themselves forward for opportunities. The development programme boosts the self-belief and confidence of ethnic minority and disabled staff by giving them feedback on their skills and helping them practise situations they will have to tackle if they are to get ahead, such as promotion interviews. In other words, the programme equips them with some of the skills they need but also boosts their belief that they have and can demonstrate all the required skills.

The programme has been very well-received by delegates. While it is a long way between putting on the programme and them applying successfully for senior level posts, there is no doubt that this programme will enable delegates to function more effectively in their current posts and it would be a great surprise if it did not result in a better representation of ethnic minority and disabled staff at senior levels than would otherwise have been the case. Assuming that this is the case, the programme will help gain traction to a virtuous circle whereby a better diversity climate generates its own ongoing successes.

Failing to act with programmes like this has the opposite effect and can help create a vicious circle that leads to the phenomenon of "corporate flight" (Hom, Roberson and Ellis, 2008) by already under-represented groups. This article by Hom et al. reported on the attrition statistics for nearly half a million American employees of mainly Fortune 500 corporations. These statistics show that the turnover of female professionals and managers is higher than that of their male counterparts and perpetuates the under-representation of women in executive positions. In turn, the lack of female exemplars at the top undermines the diversity climate and contributes to women's higher rates of quitting. The same vicious circle also applied to ethnic minorities who were shown to suffer slower career progress than white male executives.

So we have people quitting because there are not people like them at the top and the more they quit the fewer there are. Breaking this loop requires overcoming some pernicious prejudices. One example is provided by recent research (Heilman and Okimoto, 2008) that demonstrated that applicants for promotion who were described as either fathers or mothers obtained lower scores than non–parents for anticipated job commitment and anticipated achievement striving. In addition, mothers, but not fathers, received lower ratings for competence than other people and fewer passed through a screening process. The authors apply the term "the maternal wall" to their findings. They suggest that mothers are particularly associated with having stereotypically female attributes and to lack the stereotypically male attributes that are associated in people's minds with success in the powerful positions in commerce.

Findings such as these should cause every leader to pause for thought and wonder if they really are making the best use of the talent available to them. We are not talking, of course, about the sort of direct or indirect discrimination that is the subject of legislation. Rather, we are dealing with the, no doubt unconscious, subtle and partial, exclusion of whole categories of people. For example, Barclays Bank (reported by Syedain, 2008) noted in 2005 that only a third of their disabled staff openly registered their disability and found that disabled staff were amongst the lowest in terms of engagement scores. The bank decided to act and set up a group chaired by the chief executive to listen to the issues faced by disabled staff and come up with solutions. The areas identified for particular attention were the recruitment of disabled people; their promotion and development; and support from line managers.

Subsequent initiatives on these three areas have transformed the bank's employment of disabled people. Particularly noteworthy is a scheme called 'Recruitment that Works' that targets disabled people for entry level jobs in call centres. These people would previously have been out of work on social welfare benefits. Instead, they are given two weeks of work preparation training and then they go through the normal recruitment process. The bank's experience of these recruits is that they become both high-performing and loyal members of staff.

The bank has also taken steps to ensure that disabled staff receive the IT help they need, paying for this through a central budget rather than it coming from individual line managers' budgets. They have also set up a mentoring scheme for the disabled, a disability portal and compulsory training for line managers. All this effort has been rewarded. The number of registered disabled has trebled and disabled staff now deliver engagement scores that are close to or higher than those of other staff.

What these initiatives illustrate is that action to bring in the excluded pays off. Action on the diversity climate goes beyond that which is strictly required by the law and it is action that might well not even occur to those of us who are able bodied, not from an ethnic minority and thoroughly included. If you listen to partially excluded groups at work it is a real eye-opener to hear things from their point of view. Apart from under-representation at senior levels, there are all the petty annoyances. People with diabetes need to eat at regular times and so meetings that run on cause them problems; colleagues go off to the bar in the evening and finish off discussing a decision, leaving excluded the Muslim who does not drink alcohol; the company intranet uses a font that the partially sighted cannot read. And so on. The best way to find out is to follow the example of the Barclays Chief Executive and talk with people.

Put more generally, in order to ensure that the full diversity of talent is considered for the organisation's talent pools it is essential to follow best practice in terms of recruiting, identifying and managing talent in all its diversity, First of all, it is important to look widely when sourcing talent rather than just making a narrow population

lacking in diversity aware of opportunities. Organisations should be actively encouraging as diverse a group of candidates to apply for their positions as possible. Second, people in all their diversity must feel welcome and encouraged to apply. Targeted recruitment advertising, promotional material highlighting a company's embracing of diversity and encouraging flexible working practices can all contribute in this way. Particularly helpful to this is to be able to display diversity affirming statements in advertisements and to have persuasive case studies of people from all demographic backgrounds succeeding in the organisation.

CHAPTER THREE

SPOTTING TALENT

THE MORE SENIOR THE ROLE, THE LESS YOU KNOW THE CHALLENGES THE CHOSEN PERSON WILL FACE BEYOND THE IMMEDIATE FUTURE

The job of selection is to identify people who can display the indicators of excellence required for the talent pool. For some pools, this might just involve the display of behaviours for immediate performance. For other pools, we want to see if someone shows the potential to display more demanding indicators, under the presumption that they will get some developmental input to help them advance. In such cases, we need to be clear what the person is eventually expected to do excellently. We then need to decide what people must be excellent at now if they are to stand a chance of developing into the excellent person of the future. Finally we have to see how well they can exhibit the 'excellent now' behaviours.

Of course, the behavioural requirements in the future will almost inevitably be different to the present because the role in the future will have altered – either a new role or an evolved role. Broadly, the further into the future that the organisation is projecting, the less certainty can there be about the behaviours people will need. Organisations must make their best estimate of future requirements based upon their strategy and keep this estimate updated.

Fundamentally, what organisations want is productive behaviour in the particular key situations that make up a job or role and people differ in their capacity and willingness to produce the behaviours that organisations want. This applies both to immediate behaviour (current performance) and behaviour to develop for the future (potential).

Capability to show behaviour in a role is best evidenced by getting the person to give an example of the behaviour in the same role. This is the approach traditionally taken to selection. Behavioural evidence is at the core of asking others about a person's capabilities to behave (in performance appraisal and references), giving the person a trial appointment (the probation period and internships), and asking about behaviour in an interview. Gathering behavioural evidence is also the heart of the assessment centre approach. It is the first approach to spotting talent to be considered in more detail.

ASSESSMENT CENTRES

Assessment centres get people to behave in a range of simulations of the role that they would perform, if appointed (Woodruffe, 2007). The more closely the simulations replicate the actual role the more certain one can be that behaviour in the role will be the same as behaviour in the simulation. Conversely, if assessment centres are no more than generic management games the predictiveness of the centre will melt away. Only tailored exercises closely resembling the target role should be part of a proper assessment centre.

Nevertheless, there are restrictions to the assessment centre approach. The most

fundamental restrictions are:

1 You cannot preview all situations, particularly because the future of the role is not entirely known.

2 People do not necessarily typically behave in the way that they can behave. They might be able but are they willing? In an assessment centre there is a very strong and clear demand, for example, to be courteous. When these strong demands are lifted, the person might well revert to a different type. Even if a behaviour is in our repertoire, we have to choose (with deliberation or not) to display it in a situation.

3 Related to the above, some situations are relatively strong in terms of behaviours they evoke (few people make jokes at a funeral); others allow more latitude (on the beach you might read a book or find someone to talk to). Still others are relatively strong but ambiguous. You know you must do something but different people have different interpretations of what is required. Some assessment centre exercises are like this – strong but ambiguous. We are clearly meant to behave in a group exercise but is it better to say little and agree with others or to advance our views forcefully? And does either choice show what we are 'really like'?

We have then two dilemmas. The obvious way of predicting behaviour in specific situations is to have a preview of behaviour in those same situations. However, firstly, some situations cannot be previewed because they are unknown. The best we can do is preview a best-estimate of the future as well as looking for behaviour that will carry a person through change and transition. Secondly, we do not know that a person who can behave with excellence will go on to do so. One answer is to ensure that performance management continues to encourage the person who can behave excellently to do so. Another is to

ensure that the previews of behaviour are sufficiently robust to afford confidence that they show the 'real person'. This means being extremely vigilant when observing people for any signs of inauthentic behaviour. It also means making the simulation exercises of adequate complexity and of sufficient length that they give less opportunity for candidates to act or put on a performance. Alternatively, we might look beyond the assessment centre and base a decision on lengthy exposure to the person – either through employment in an internship or through regular employment using references and performance appraisal.

INTERNSHIPS

An Internship can be seen as an extended assessment centre. It gives the organisation a wonderful opportunity to assess the intern's capability in precisely the situations that he or she would confront if offered permanent employment. Thinking this through, it is clear that internships need to be carefully structured if they are to offer maximum advantage. In particular, it is important that the intern is:

1 Shown the 'tricks of the trade' to enable them to reveal their maximum performance capability. It would be foolish to lose sight of someone's talent because they have not been given basic training in how to perform tasks.

2 Put in situations that will demonstrate their capability to perform – the situations need to be realistic for their experience but also demanding.

3 Assessed objectively and in a disciplined way. Those supervising the intern should be trained in the same skills as assessment centre assessors (the assessment skills they need, anyway, as managers of people) and asked to provide reports against the indicators of excellence. The reporting process might also be extended to others with whom the intern interacts ('peers', support staff etc).

INTERVIEWS

A behavioural interview has the objective of questioning the person about their demonstration of the indicators of excellence. The interview has the obvious advantage that it is based on potentially a lifetime's sample of the person's behaviour but it also has the three disadvantages detailed on the next page.

1 The interviewee will naturally try to select favourable examples and leave aside the less favourable. A recent article by Julia Levashina and Michael Campion (2007) showed than no less than 95 per cent of undergraduate job candidates fake during employment interviews. Although there is some encouragement from the fact that a smaller percentage than this "engage in faking behaviors that are semantically closer to lying", that still leaves virtually every graduate engaging in 'Slight Image Creation' and 'Ingratiation'.

The researchers looked at eleven facets of faking and found the following:

64% engage in Constructing
– defined as 'to build stories by combining or arranging work experiences to provide better answers'

75% engage in Inventing
– defined as 'to cook up better answers', such as claiming work experiences they did not have.

34% engage in Borrowing
– defined as 'to answer based on the experiences or accomplishments of others'.

2 Apart from conscious 'faking' behaviour, candidates who are highly articulate tend to do much better than those who are not so articulate.

3 The role for which the person is being considered might contain novel elements and requirements that cannot be anticipated from past behaviour. This can be a particular problem when recruiting graduates with little past experience but high potential. The situational interview is an alternative to the behavioural interview in these circumstances. Candidates are asked hypothetical questions of what they might do in situations typical to those faced on the job. However, candidates are even more likely to 'fake' their responses to these kind of questions than they are to questions based on past behaviour. Also, it has been suggested that those who do well on situational interviews are actually just better at problem-solving skills – in this case solving the problem of what is the best response.

Recent research by Paul Derek Martin and John Pope (2008) has also suggested that the focus on eliciting evidence of behaviour should not be the sole reason for an interview. They stress the importance of exploring people's approach to work by examining factors such as their willingness to learn and adapt, which are also more future-proofed qualities.

In summary, interviewing someone about their behaviour is inherently less accurate as a means of assessing capability than actually seeing the person's behaviour. However, it might be used very effectively in conjunction with observing action to understand the reasons for and typicality of actions.

APPRAISALS

If you are seeking to assess current employees against the indicators of excellence, the obvious starting point is to collect all the evidence you have in the form of an appraisal of them. This might employ multi-raters in the form of 360-degree appraisal.

Unfortunately, appraisal has some well–known drawbacks:

- Raters are often generous, inaccurate and inconsistent with each other. These problems can become even greater if an appraisal is being specifically conducted for the purpose of selection. Candour declines and the consequence of this are obviously grave in terms of promoting the wrong people.

- The behaviours of interest may not have been called for in the past and so cannot be the subject of an appraisal.

However, rather than abandon this potentially rich source of information, we would advocate some or all of the following:

- Training appraisers in the task of observing and rating behaviour.

- Asking for evidence to support the ratings. This can either be written evidence or it can be elicited through an interview with the appraiser.

- Imposing on the rater the need to choose between people, such as by using forced-choice rankings.

REFERENCES

References perform the same role with external candidates as appraisals do for internals. Unfortunately they also suffer from all the problems of appraisal, with the only strengthening measure being to ask for evidence for the referee's opinions. This can be done, for example by using a structured reference form asking for a mixture of ratings and written responses to specific questions. References also suffer from the potential problems of referees being wary of the legal repercussions of their references and of them not being particularly motivated to provide the time and effort that a reference can entail. Generally, the person being reported on has left and is owed only the minimum in terms of a reference.

Despite these limitations, there will be circumstances where references are a useful way forward. In the work we did on the system for awarding Queen's Counsel (QC) status to advocates, we made extensive use of references by judges, professional peers and clients to gauge a person's excellence at advocacy. In the academic world, it is commonplace to take up references before making a selection decision. As a generalisation, it can be seen that the closer referees can be considered colleagues of those requesting the references, and the reference therefore mimics an appraisal, the more viable references become.

PSYCHOMETRIC TESTS AND INVENTORIES

Ability tests and personality inventories measure the broader behavioural domain that the work capability belongs to. Tests of reasoning or intelligence get the person to demonstrate behaviours while personality inventories get people to self-report behaviours – in both cases behaviours at a relatively general level. The behaviours that are demonstrated or self-reported are taken to be indicative of a general ability or trait that determines the person's propensity to display the behaviour that the organisation wants.

The measure of general reasoning appears to broaden the range of situations in which the person can demonstrate their being capable of behaving in the desired way. Ideally a self-report of typical behaviour from a personality inventory would do the same and provide reassurance that the person typically behaves in the way that they have shown they are capable of behaving at the assessment centre. It should give an indication of how the person prefers or is disposed to behave, combining both ability and willingness to behave that way. If answered honestly and accurately, the personality inventory might give valuable information.

However, inventories have the extreme limitation that people vary a great deal between situations and so the indices of typical behaviour provided by personality inventories might well be very poor predictors of behaviour in specific situations. It would be somewhat naïve to measure personality and hope that a particular profile will lead to the desired behaviours in specific situations. Furthermore, personality inventories are unlikely to yield useful additional information for selection because they are so susceptible to distortion. No doubt, because of these limitations, personality inventories typically have trivial levels of validity for predicting job performance.

NEUROPSYCHOLOGICAL TESTS

A tempting option is to measure the individual differences that are the causes of behaviour – both the behaviour seen at the assessment centre and reported upon in the personality inventory. In theory, we could try and go right back to measuring differences in the brain. But it is inconceivable that it would ever be acceptable to measure people's brain differences even if this was theoretically desirable. In the case of ability, measuring differences in the brain does not seem to add anything to measuring differences in what the brain can do as shown by reasoning and intelligence tests. In the case of personality, it is clear that physiology is only a partial cause of differences in behaviour and one that interacts with learning to cause behaviour.

DEPTH PSYCHOLOGY

Organisations want to see indicators of excellence – i.e., behaviours. At selection, essentially the choice is between measuring the behaviours directly or measuring the antecedents of the behaviours. For example, behaviour is the product of key schemas such as attachment beliefs that cause some people to behave in a secure manner when others become anxious or withdrawn. We might gauge people's attachment and infer what their behaviour will be. We might also measure values and preferences. However, the limitation is that there will never be a one-to-one established correspondence between these background variables and the particular behaviours the organisation wants to acquire. Returning to Figure 3, the particular behaviour of a particular person in a particular situation depends on a host of variables and it would be entirely impractical for organisations to try to predict by measuring those variables. Furthermore, although, we can work backwards from the behaviours to their antecedents it is virtually impossible to work forwards. How could one possibly apply a formula to the raw materials of behaviour to predict specific behaviours in specific situations? For all practical purposes one could not.

THE WAY FORWARD

The only practical way to select people is to preview their behaviour in the role. As Figure 6 illustrates, the closer you get to what you are predicting, the more accurate is the prediction likely to be.

	Internal Staff	External Recruitment
DIRECT	Appraisal Assessment Centres	Internships Assessment Centres
INDIRECT	Interviews Ability tests Personality inventories	Interviews Ability tests Personality inventories References
INFERRED	Depth psychology Neuropsychology	Depth psychology Neuropsychology

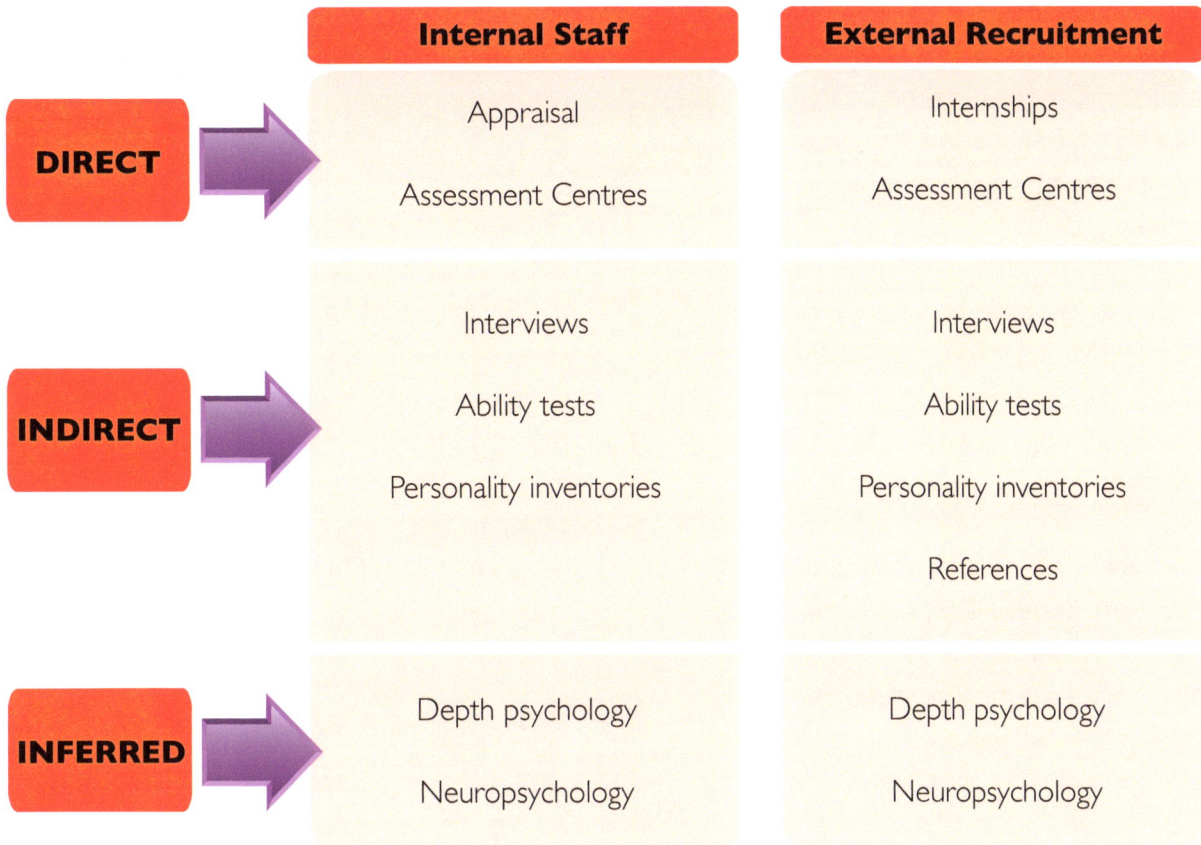

Figure 6. Getting close to what you are predicting

FIT WITH THE ORGANISATION AND TEAM

As described above, the ability to perform is only part of the equation. Motivation also plays a big part and fit with the organisation and team are key considerations. Organisations are involved in different activities, have different values and work in different ways. Individuals also have different values and preferences. Research and practice tell us that when individuals' and organisations'

values and styles align, employees are much more motivated to perform and go the extra mile in their jobs. Any selection procedure should pay attention to this in the interview or through the use of a values questionnaire.

If a person is going to be working predominantly within a certain team, compatibility with that team is also important and person-team fit should be checked in a selection process.

THE STRATEGIC IMPORTANCE OF ASSESSMENT

Accurate assessment comes at a price. It is a price that will seem prohibitive if managers are not taken through the strategic logic of accurately identifying talent. On the other hand, it should seem well worth paying to those who are clear on where it fits within the talent strategy and who see the line of sight through the talent strategy to the business strategy of winning by having the best people.

Assessment plays a part in all components of a talent strategy. Most obviously, it should deliver the best people to fill vacancies and gaps in the leadership pipeline. However, just as importantly, it is vital for allocating development and engaging the best people. To attract and retain talented people, organisations must set about meeting their needs. However, clearly, not everybody can be offered the maximum satisfaction of all possible needs. Meeting people's needs involves allocating scarce resources. The people offered the most inducements to stay must be the truly talented. Otherwise you will end up retaining the 'wrong' people.

In addition, to get any commitment from people organisations must commit to them. Such a strategy of commitment and partnership implies that forming the relationship is done with the utmost care. Both sides need to maximize their information about each other. Mistakes cannot be afforded on the employer's side if a commitment has been made. If the employee feels they made a mistake and leaves, the cost is the loss of organisational investment and having to recruit the replacement.

There is a huge range in the estimated cost of turnover. A guide by the CIPD (2008) puts the figure at £20,000 for senior managers and directors, based upon a survey of members. Other estimates are much higher but even the CIPD estimate is an inducement to invest in accurate assessment to avoid the penalties. Put starkly, without the investment, organisations risk the penalty of turnover by choosing the wrong people and losing the best people.

DIVERSITY

With the selection process, it is essential to have guidelines in place on selecting people from the talent pool, based on suitable criteria, otherwise the process is subject to bias and the diversity of the candidates may be put at risk. Indeed, recent research has highlighted some important examples of selection procedures being biased against certain groups of candidates. For example, black applicants seeking voluntary work in organisations found that they faced more rejection than white applicants in a study by Howitt and Owusu–Bempah (1990).

Worryingly, it has also been suggested by Pyburn, Ployart and Kravitz (2008) that the best selection procedures for predicting future job performance, i.e. the most valid, are also often those where different ethnic or gender groups perform significantly differently. The prime example is cognitive ability tests, where significant differences have been found between the performance of different ethnic groups. This needs to be borne in mind when using such methods. One way of reducing the impact of the potential discrimination caused by such methods is to use them in combination with a range of other measures.

Unstructured interviews also increase bias in selection settings and so potentially threaten diversity. Structured interviews are preferable. In a recent seminar on the topic of diversity in the workplace, Jo Silvester (2008) reported findings that women were typically asked more closed questions (requiring short or yes/no answers) and were given less opportunity to talk than male candidates, findings that reinforce the need for standardised interviews. Beginning an interview with a discussion of a candidate's culture can additionally be helpful in breaking down stereotypes which might affect how the interviewer interprets the answers to the rest of their questions, according to Lim and colleagues (2006).

Of course, even if selection procedures themselves are conducted in a diversity-friendly way, the way candidates are assessed in those procedures can still be subject to diversity issues. As we have already mentioned, traditional competencies can be limiting in terms of diversity and encourage cloning. However, Indicators of Excellence specify the final output needed for high performance and recognise that different people will reach that final output in different ways. Nevertheless, the indicators should be diversity-proofed with a particular emphasis on ensuring that they do not represent just one group's view of what success in the role means and that they use language that is neutral with respect to gender, ethnicity etc.

CHAPTER FOUR

DEVELOPING TALENT

YOU CAN ONLY HOPE TO KEEP PEOPLE BY ENABLING THEM TO LEAVE

To be recognised as a top employer or an Investor in People, you must offer good development opportunities. Development is the biggest contributor to active talent management and operates in two ways.

1) It increases your stock of human capital. You develop people to make the most of their talent and maximize their capability. Development must address why important behaviours that are required now are not being displayed and this will call for diagnostic skill. Development will also help people acquire the behaviours required for the future.

Failing to invest in people's ongoing development almost inevitably means that gradually their value will diminish and so they will offer the organisation less. For people without experience, the arguments are all the more obvious. If high potential staff are seen as a strategic response to the future, it is axiomatic that one nurtures them to increase their value and preparation.

2) Development helps retain people by meeting key needs. In particular, it enables them to maintain their employability and the sense that they are growing and moving forwards. It also signals a commitment to them.

These two reasons for a development strategy – increasing the stock of human capital and retaining people by meeting their needs are intertwined. Talent development sets up a virtuous circle. By developing people you both increase their capability and offer a powerful reason for people to stay by meeting their need to be developed.

However, despite their being interlinked, each reason gives rise to a different set of priorities and considerations to be borne in mind when deciding on a development intervention. Pinpointing why you are developing your employees can help you answer the questions of what exactly to develop, who to develop and how to develop them. Figure 7 works through the flow of thinking once you clarify the prime reason why you are developing people.

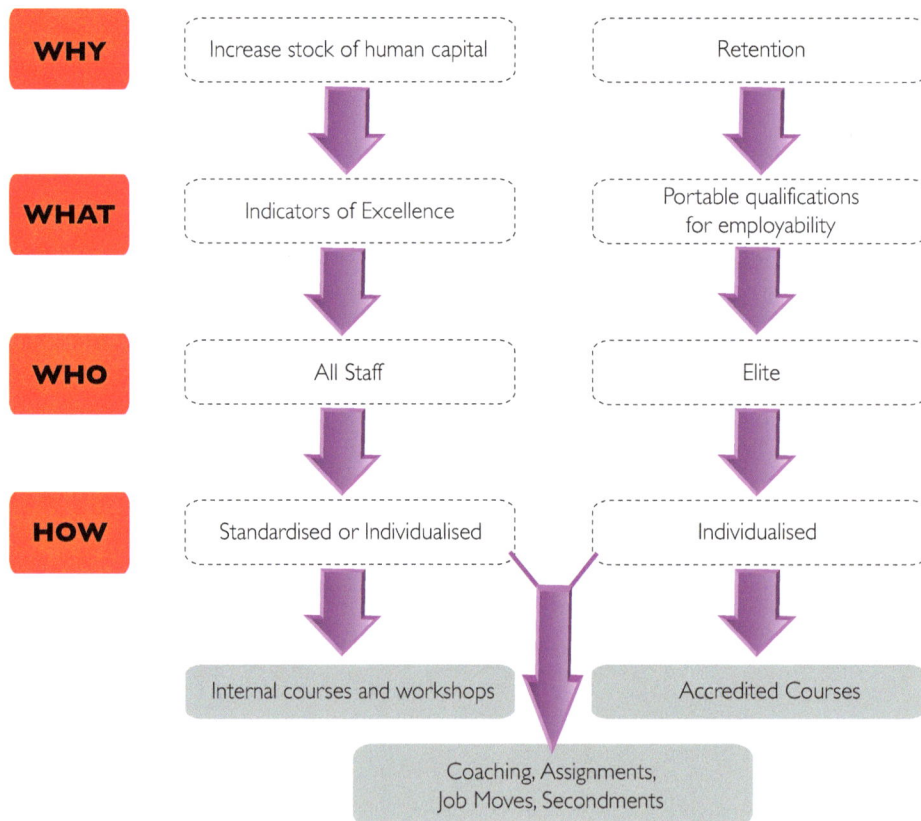

WHY	Increase stock of human capital	Retention
WHAT	Indicators of Excellence	Portable qualifications for employability
WHO	All Staff	Elite
HOW	Standardised or Individualised	Individualised
	Internal courses and workshops	Accredited Courses
	Coaching, Assignments, Job Moves, Secondments	

Figure 7. The development flow chart

WHAT

If development is primarily to increase your human capital, you want employees to develop skills that will enable them to add more value to the business, both now and in the future. However, if you are approaching development from the standpoint of retention, they should have more choice as to what kind of skills they would like to develop, and these are likely to be transferable skills which are marketable. In reality of course, a development strategy will take both strands into account, but there may be more of an emphasis on the one or the other at any point in time.

If we take the perspective of increasing your human capital, you need to determine the development needs of your employees in relation to business needs. The Indicators of Excellence approach keeps development needs focused on your business strategy. This focus on the business strategy helps to pinpoint areas of development of high priority far more easily than competencies. For example, to achieve the company goal of becoming a major retailer, customer-facing employees need to learn to be impeccable at putting the customer first.

If the main focus for a development activity is to retain talent a good place to start would be to consult with your employees on what development they want. This process of involving employees should ensure buy-in to the development activities and more importantly, sends the message that the

organisation is interested in employees' wants – of utmost importance if your goal is to retain people.

For retention through employability, the focus for development will be generic behaviours, such as communication or management skills – skills which would be attractive to another employer as well as to your organisation. The precise focus of development will differ depending on the employee, some developing on a leadership route with others developing on a professional route.

WHO

Increasing the stock of human capital applies to all staff. Of course, the development to increase human capital will be different for different talent pools and, in each case, retention will be a side benefit. On the other hand, if the focus is retention it applies particularly to the élite. The élite is synonymous with difficulty of replacement. The less replaceable someone is, the more important is their retention.

Development to increase the stock of human capital will target the indicators of excellence that each talent pool should display. As a consultancy, we believe the bias should be over – rather than under-provision of development. This is the opposite to the bias advocated by Peter Cappelli (2008) who suggests that organisations should avoid the error of developing too many people for their eventual leadership requirements or of finding that the template against which people have been developed is overtaken by events. One of the key ideas of his 'just in time' approach to talent management is that oversupply is more expensive than undersupply so you should aim to develop-from-within the lowest likely number that will be needed. You then hire additional people from outside, as they are required.

However, we believe that planning the supply of emerging talent has to be done in a continual three-way dialogue between the needs of the business, the talent manager and the people being developed. People in the process of development are not like widgets on a shelf, lying idle until their moment comes. They are human capital that should be managed to make a maximum contribution throughout the time of their development. It is fallacious to see development in the binary terms of wasted or not wasted. Rather development should be continually adjusted and utilised to the best advantage of the business.

Our preferred bias towards over-provision will also spread the net of retention. A narrow focus of development just for a select few high flyers in each talent pool is a dangerous strategy as it loses the side benefit of retention. Repeatedly having to make external appointments will clearly demotivate people who are talented and important but outside the narrow talent pool. It sends out a message that you value them less and are less committed to them, which no doubt will cause them to be

less committed to you, and increase their propensity to leave. Unlike Cappelli, we would not see development as wasted if those you have developed subsequently leave. It will enhance people's performance in their roles while they are with you, give clear messages about your commitment to people's growth and emphasise your intention to resource internally.

HOW

A more individualised approach to development has been growing rapidly in popularity amongst organisations. This encompasses a variety of development methods, most notably coaching. Previously, there was much more emphasis on training courses being 'imposed' on employees in a broad brush fashion but nowadays it is obvious how inappropriate this is, especially to busy senior leaders. The shift of focus to individualised development sees individuals having more responsibility for their own learning, is more 'on-the-job' and is in contrast to a standardised training course where employees are told exactly what they should be learning from the sessions.

The benefits of these types of individualised development over standardised training courses are that they can be tailored to individual learners and their needs and there will be a more obvious transfer of learning to relevant work situations. Whereas a training course may include useful knowledge and skills for a person's work (depending on the subject of the training) these benefits are not always immediately obvious and may be long forgotten by the time it is necessary to implement them. Learning 'on the job' however, allows employees to learn and practise skills first hand and gain real experience from the outset.

Having said this, there are, of course, situations where formalised training is still the best option. Going back to why you want to develop your employees, if the answer to this question is that you want them to be behaving in line with a revised company strategy, then a first step might be to send them on a training course to learn to implement points of your strategy (e.g., customer focus, diversity or lean production) in a time – and cost-effective manner. Development of skills dealt with on the training course would then be continued through line-manager monitoring and appraisal.

COACHING

Coaching has increased rapidly in popularity over the last few years. As an illustration, over 60 per cent of respondents to a recent survey from the CIPD (2007) reported that they use coaching in their organisations. Coaching can take many different forms, from line managers coaching their employees as part of their management role to an external coach helping an employee push past a fear of, say, making presentations to large audiences. Often line manager coaching crosses the boundary into mentoring, where guidance and support is given to the employee being coached. 'Pure' coaching does not involve giving guidance, but is focused on asking the right questions and using particular techniques based on approaches such as neuro linguistic programming (NLP) and cognitive behavioural therapy (CBT) to facilitate the person being coached in coming up with effective solutions. It is also future – and goal-focused and does not explore the past (this would be counselling rather than coaching).

The choice between internal and external coaches has several dimensions apart from cost and a summary of the advantages and disadvantages of the two options is provided in Table 2 below.

INTERNAL COACHES	EXTERNAL COACHES
Have knowledge of company culture	Have exposure to environments outside the organisation's culture, bringing in fresh approaches and experiences
Are readily available and 'known'	Have to be sourced and tested
Present a smaller cost than external coaches	Can be expensive
Might raise suspicions of confidentiality	Are perceived as objective; Can build trust with a coachee more quickly

Table 2. Internal and external coaches

Coaching can be ongoing, especially if conducted internally by a line manager, or a specific programme of coaching can be arranged, which might last, say, for six sessions.

A main advantage of using coaching over other development methods is that a good coach is motivating and brings about long-term change. Recent research undertaken by Human Assets also suggests that employees receiving coaching become more satisfied in their jobs compared to before coaching and are more likely to stay in the organisation,

even when they had been thinking about leaving.

On the other hand, not every development need lends itself to coaching, and not everyone is easily coached. There is also the problem of finding a good coach in the first place. Coaching's growth in popularity has produced an abundance of coaches of differing standards. These are some questions, published by the CIPD (2005), which we find useful to consider when selecting a coach.

✓ Do they belong to a professional body and are they supervised?

✓ What is their coaching experience and are they qualified?

✓ What is the coach's track record of success?

✓ Do they have relevant business or industry experience?

✓ Does the coach have a clear coaching process?

✓ Do they use proven coaching models and approaches?

✓ Does the coach ask you to clarify what you want or expect from the coaching process?

✓ How do they monitor progress and quality?

✓ What are their rapport skills like?

✓ Does the coach fit in with your organisation?

ASSIGNMENTS, JOB MOVES AND SECONDMENTS

There is a lot of evidence to suggest that people learn the most from experiencing challenging situations. These might be as simple as being asked to run a small project or as major as being sent on an international assignment. Whatever the scale, the objective

is for the person to develop by exposure to new demands.

When setting an assignment, there are important things to bear in mind:

● The assignment needs to be challenging to stretch the employee, but not too difficult or unachievable. This could cause the employee to lose faith in their abilities, to the obvious detriment of current and future learning.

- For the assignment to have maximum impact, it is important to offer high quality and well-delivered feedback.

- If you are preparing an employee for a future role, it would be particularly useful to set an assignment around the typicalities of that role.

Job moves and secondments work in a similar way to assignments by creating challenges from which employees can develop.

Assignments and projects need not necessarily be set in the workplace at all. For certain skills, for example project management, voluntary work in the community can bring about similar learning experiences, and might be linked, for example, to a corporate social responsibility (CSR) initiative.

SELF–AWARENESS

Whatever the development activity, self-awareness, both beforehand and afterwards, helps ensure the maximum benefit is obtained. The objective is to encourage people to realise for themselves where they need to develop, rather than simply being told. This self-awareness allows employees to go into any development activity with purpose and goals and also makes it easier

for them to recognise when development is having an effect. It also gives people more ownership of their learning.

It is important, therefore, not only that employees are aware of the Indicators of Excellence for their role and know how they are currently performing in relation to these (e.g. through regular performance appraisals or 360 degree feedback), but also that they are aware of the patterns of behaviours they have which enhance or decrease their ability to achieve these indicators of excellence. Development centres (Woodruffe, 2007) are aimed at providing a powerful opportunity for people to refine their understanding of their strengths and development needs in relation to the requirements of their current and / or future roles. Development centres use simulations like assessment centres but can also incorporate pure development sessions (e.g. on giving and receiving feedback). Development centres also frequently incorporate psychometric tools. These tools should give an increased understanding by the individual of the origins of their strengths and development needs. Referring once again to Figure 3, they are working back from the indicators of excellence to the sources of the indicators in their particular case.

TECHNOLOGY IN DEVELOPMENT

The use of technology in development has been growing steadily. Many major organisations now have some form of e-learning and some are taking this a step further and making such development tools available on portable devices such as the iPod and iPhone through audio and visual media. E-learning obviously has benefits in terms of reduced cost and increased convenience. It also allows employees to slot in their development time when it suits them and their schedules. With e-learning becoming available on portable devices too, this convenience can extend to learning on the move, an opportunity to use otherwise wasted time profitably.

E-learning does however have significant limitations. It can never fully substitute a face-to-face learning environment and is probably best used as a supportive addition to face-to-face or 'on-the-job' learning, for example as an introduction before training or consolidation afterwards. From a learning point of view, interactivity is of importance if e-learning is to have an impact. Indeed, organisations that use e-learning are taking this on board and embracing new interactive computer-game technology to enhance their e-learning systems. Volvo even use a computer game to help sales staff improve their sales techniques with virtual customers, as described by a recent article by Eyre (2007). Taking this one step further, an increasing number of large firms are creating environments on the virtual reality world on the internet. Second Life allows employees to log on and interact with the learning materials as a virtual person (an avatar) and interact with others, similar to instant messaging but where you can 'see' the person you are talking to (or at least their

virtual alter-ego).

If one of the aims of development is to show commitment to your employees, you need to be very careful about the way you introduce e-learning and portable learning to your organisation. Poorly communicated, such initiatives could give your employees the impression that development is not high on your priority list, only allowing time to squeeze it in between other pieces of work or even travelling between business meetings. On the other hand, phrased differently, using such technology could indicate that you are investing in your employees by giving them maximum opportunity to access learning resources.

LEARNING THEORY

For learning to occur, there are consecutive stages that a learner needs to go through, represented by the Kolb Learning Cycle (Kolb, 1984). Simply put, stage one is actually having the experience; then people need to reflect on, draw conclusions from and try out what they have learned.

In any development programme, it is important to consider how to facilitate each stage of the learning cycle. For example, give learners the experiences they need to learn and then prompt reflection through self-appraisal.

Research suggests that there are four types of learner, each having significantly different preferences in the way they like to learn and

Activists Enjoy learning through experience	**Reflectors** Prefer to spend a long time reflecting	**Theorists** Like to make connections and form ideas from their experiences	**Pragmatists** Prefer to plan

feel they get the most out of learning. These are related to the stages of the learning cycle. The four types are the activists, reflectors, theorists and the pragmatists.

With a focus on individual, self-directed development, there is more room for tailoring the style of learning to each employee according to their preferred learning styles. Tailoring individual employees' learning in light of their preferences will be much more productive than a 'one size fits all' approach. Ensuring that non-tailored development activities include a range of activities suited to different learning styles is also recommended to make sure each employee is learning at some time in a style which suits them.

GENERATIONAL DIFFERENCES

There may also be differences between the generations in terms of the most appropriate modes of learning. Members of what is popularly called 'Generation Y' (roughly speaking, those born between 1980 and 1995) have largely grown up in a world of computer games and 'e-communication', and

may well be more familiar and comfortable with this technology in a developmental perspective than previous generations. For some, particularly the younger generation, increasing use of technology is seen as innovative and positive, whereas for others it could be seen as an unnecessary gimmick, which is inferior to more traditional developmental activities.

Employees who fall into the Generation Y bracket typically place higher importance on the development of transferable skills than previous generations and Generation Y is caricatured as moving frequently between organisations and job roles. It may be worth considering, then, the increased use of individualised development activities which focus on retaining employees, such as assignments and coaching under the maxim that people will only stay if you enable them to leave. Playing up development activities unique to your organisation such as assignments may also encourage Generation Y employees to stay in your organisation.

ENGAGING TALENT

YOU PARTICULARLY WANT TO KEEP THE VERY PEOPLE WHO HAVE THE ABILITY AND GUMPTION TO GO

Talented people nowadays have a clear notion of their value to employers: Indeed, and especially in a recession, some 'marginal talent' might overestimate their indispensability. This is understandable as until the end of 2008 employers were falling over each other in the war for talent. Anecdotally, the image that went the rounds with graduates was 'They'll do anything to get you'. And, in many respects, employers should still be doing so. It is talented people who will enable organisations to win through in difficult economic times.

Of course, the reality might be that organisations have to put a punctuation mark in their pipeline of recruitment of talent. However, they would be well-advised to do all they can to ensure that they retain the talent they already have on board. How they will do so is, in essence, stated quite simply. You will win the war for talent by meeting people's needs better than your competitors. It is a simple answer but it is also difficult because you have to identify those needs; be able to meet them; and recognise that people discover new needs as your competitors offer to satisfy them.

The meeting of people's needs has given rise to a new marketing-based language. The *employment proposition* sums up what is on offer and the *employer brand* describes the overall concept of being employed by one organisation rather than another. However, at the heart of these ideas is the identification and satisfaction of people's needs at work.

For simplicity, people's needs can be arranged under the three headings of the package, employability and satisfaction, as illustrated in Figure 8. This is not perfect science but it does offer a way of ordering the needs people have.

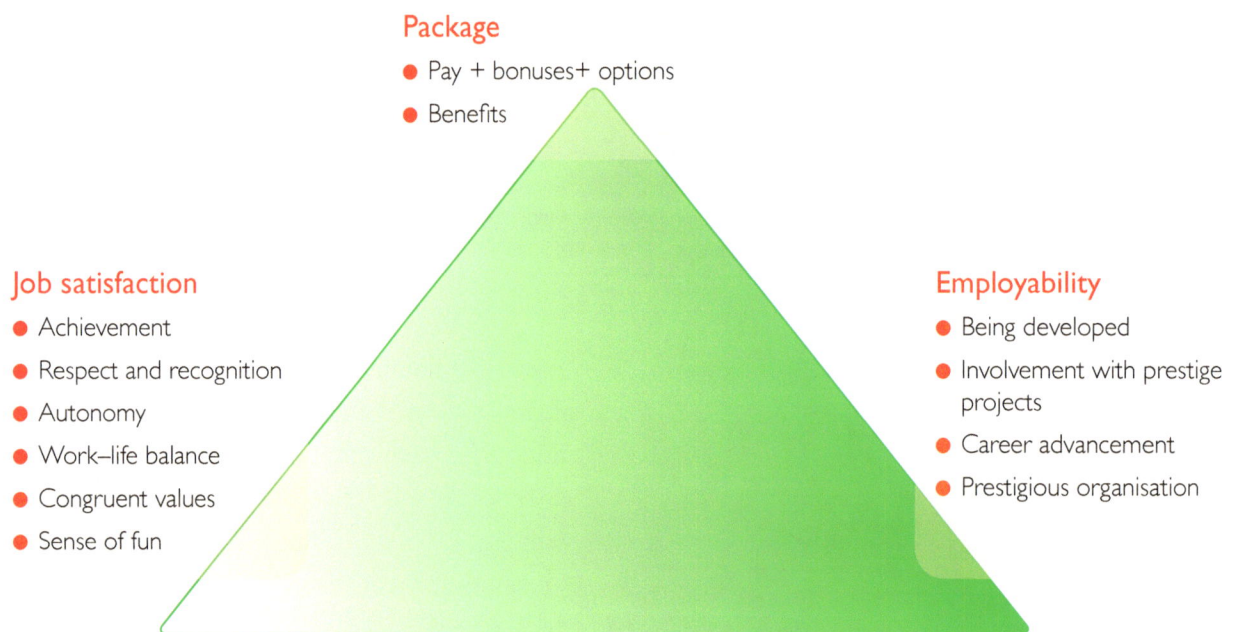

Package
- Pay + bonuses+ options
- Benefits

Job satisfaction
- Achievement
- Respect and recognition
- Autonomy
- Work–life balance
- Congruent values
- Sense of fun

Employability
- Being developed
- Involvement with prestige projects
- Career advancement
- Prestigious organisation

Figure 8. The engagement triangle

The entire triangle must be considered if organisations are to attract and retain talented people – if they are to be *employers of choice*. What is more, people must be treated as individuals. For example, some people want to sacrifice pay for more holidays in their package; for others it is the other way round.

Taking the three components of the triangle in turn, there are several specific factors to consider for each of them.

THE PACKAGE

To be an employer of choice, people must be paid equitably. Their sense of fairness will be undermined by invidious comparisons both within their organisation and externally. They want to see a reasonable payback for the value they create.

However, although the package is a vital component towards being an employer of choice, few people flock to an otherwise bad employer purely because they pay well and, generally, the package is the least sure way of retaining people for it is the inducement that is most easily matched by another employer. Competitors that offer to meet the other needs of staff as well as the package will have the winning proposition.

EMPLOYABILITY

We do not go to work just to earn today's money, but tomorrow's also. People are concerned with an income stream rather than just immediate money. They want employability.

There are four major factors that affect employability:

1 BEING DEVELOPED

As the last chapter made clear, talented people nowadays demand development. They recognise that the future is uncertain and even a committed employer cannot guarantee a job. They want to be ready with a passport to alternative employment. Organisations must give a high priority to people's development in order to retain them and to attract them in the first place. Development must cover both people's professional skills and also their skills to be a manager/leader. Some of the development will be by courses and workshops. However, as noted, the most powerful development comes from providing people with new experiences, particularly experiences that challenge them.

2 INVOLVEMENT WITH PRESTIGE PROJECTS

Ambitious people, notably today's Generation Y graduates, like visibility. They relish the opportunity to tackle prestigious projects, particularly those that will give exposure to people with power in the organisation. Assuming their contribution is a positive one, such exposure enhances employability.

3 CAREER ADVANCEMENT

Drive and motivation is part of what makes a person talented – a high-flyer. Advancement feeds their goal of securing and maintaining an income stream. Part of the image of being an employer of choice comes from letting good people get ahead quickly.

Of course, an organisation should not be offering people a guaranteed or perfectly defined route forwards. Progress depends upon people's development. However, high-flyers want to see the possibilities for advancement.

4 BEING PART OF A PRESTIGIOUS ORGANISATION

There is an advantage to the employee in working for a prestigious organisation that is at the leading edge of its sector. It has a currency on the job market and is extremely good experience for a curriculum vitae. The experience will generate future income. The importance of this factor is clear from organisations' thirst to be among the list of Top 100 employers (e.g., The Times Top 100 Graduate Employers).

JOB SATISFACTION

If people go out to work to generate the income for a style of life, they also want to be happy whilst doing so. The importance of job satisfaction becomes particularly obvious when one is trying to attract and retain people who do not need money.

For example, Microsoft was, at one stage, estimated to employ 9,000 millionaires. Many of the millionaires who go to work do so, presumably, because it is satisfying rather than out of a need for income per se or employability. Six components of job satisfaction can be separated:

1 A SENSE OF ACHIEVEMENT

To be an employer of choice, you want your staff to be telling their friends about the tremendous achievements they have notched up, not how they are bored out of their brains and underutilised.

2 A SENSE OF BEING OF RESPECTED AND RECOGNISED

People are less tolerant than in the past of status distinctions and barriers. They want to be trusted with information and to have their hard work noticed. People's sense of being respected, praised and recognised depends upon the style of their immediate manager. Some managers give praise and recognition. Others give feedback that consists mainly of telling people about the small things they have done wrong rather than large things they have done right. Raising managers' skill is vital to being an employer of choice.

3 A SENSE OF AUTONOMY

People enjoy a sense of autonomy and of being trusted to get on and deliver. They can be frustrated if they do not feel a sense of ownership over their projects or if they lack real responsibility. It was partly satisfying this sense of autonomy that made 'dot coms' so attractive a decade ago and that larger organisations tried to mimmick with 'incubators'.

4 A NEED FOR BALANCE BETWEEN THEIR WORK AND THEIR PRIVATE LIFE

Today's graduates are said to be motivated by a need for balance between their work and their private life. Of course, there are still plenty of examples of ambitious people sacrificing the balance, notably in the finance sector. They are probably quite happy to do so. Indeed, Goldman Sachs, the number one large employer in 2007 and number three the following year has the realistic job preview on their website emphasising the "fast-paced, high-energy environment" in which all their recruits will work. However, organisations should be mindful that there will be many prized employees for whom balance is a priority. It is important to avoid a culture of 'presenteeism' and look for opportunities to enable people to achieve balance, for example, by granting their requests to 'work from home'.

5 ## CONGRUENT VALUES

People want to work in an organisation with values that are congruent with those of themselves and their friends. By definition, values are something on which we differ. However, at any period of time there is a dominant value system with which employers would be better off being congruent than discordant. For example, nowadays, organisations strive to parade their 'corporate social responsibility' credentials and this must be for their staff to witness as much as their customers.

6 ## A SENSE OF FUN IN A GOOD WORKING ENVIRONMENT

Many people prefer to work in an atmosphere that is informal and fun. Organisations have sought to meet this in all sorts of ways, such as by having trendy office environments, 'dress-down' days and team-building events of various sorts.

AN INFLATION OF NEEDS

Broadly speaking, talented people will be attracted and retained by your organisation to the extent that you meet their needs. The problem is that everyone else is also trying to meet their needs and there is an inflation in people's expectations of what they want and might reasonably expect to receive. Just as we never knew we absolutely had to have mobile phones, the internet and air conditioned offices, so staff in the past never knew they absolutely have to have career breaks, major responsibilities in their twenties and to be on first name terms with an approachable CEO. So your task is to meet the needs of talented people better than the next organisation. This competition to meet people's needs is seen by some writers to have ushered in a new era of non-unionised labour power. Capital will compete to secure talented people as long as there is still a profit left: Indeed the only way

of making a profit long-term is to pay the rate for talented people. Somehow, this inflation does not show up vividly in government economic statistics but we see it only too clearly in the packages – let alone the other needs – of the CEOs and Directors of FTSE Companies. What we do not see are the costs incurred by other employees for their career breaks, MBAs, hiring two people to do one job etc., all of which are laudable but all of which come with a price.

In short, talented people have upped the stakes in the talent war. Certainly the image of Generation Y is of particularly choosy people dedicated single mindedly to their careers. Getting them to stay will be a tall order and you will have to be sure that you hit all the right buttons in getting them to join you for even a brief visit.

WINNING THE TALENT WAR: IS BIGGER BETTER OR SMALL BEAUTIFUL?

To what extent does the size of organisation matter to winning the talent war? Does the global corporation have an advantage by being able to offer overseas postings and big company benefits or is the small company more enticing by offering talented people immediate influence and closeness to the centres of power? Looking at the various needs in the triangle, Table 3 makes some comments on the comparison between larger and smaller organisations.

	LARGE VERSUS SMALL	COMMENT
PACKAGE PAY + BONUSES + OPTIONS BENEFITS	No necessary advantage for any size. For example small hedge funds might well pay more than their large finance sector rivals. Larger organisations appear better placed to offer an array of in house benefits (e.g., company gym and restaurant), but smaller organisations could offer tailored benefits that are outsourced (membership of local gym etc).	You have to pay an equitable amount. Any sized organisation might be able to trade some element of pay for the other needs (e.g., lower pay in small organisation but more flexible working or lower pay in a large organisation but better name for c.v.). However, some people will go just for the money.
EMPLOYABILITY BEING DEVELOPED	Larger organisations clearly have more opportunity for formal training and development and have an advantage in terms of being able to offer a range of development opportunities. However, small organisations can subscribe to external recognised training and are at no disadvantage in terms of offering individual development, particularly coaching, that is in keeping with contemporary thinking.	Organisations cannot hope to retain good people without developing them. Small organisations have to offer the same overall development opportunities as their larger rivals.

INVOLVEMENT WITH PRESTIGE PROJECTS	Almost by definition, large organisations have more such projects. Although small organisations have greater opportunity for access to directors, they are less able to offer projects that will enhance a CV.	
CAREER ADVANCEMENT	Large organisations might be in a better position to offer the range of experience and support necessary for people to achieve professional qualifications. However, this is by no means their exclusive advantage and small organisations can offer more rapid advancement in terms of offering responsibilities and seniority.	Small organisations must ensure that they support professional advancement. Large organisations must be flexible in terms of offering promotion on merit rather than insisting on people waiting their turn or a certain period of time before moving up.
PRESTIGIOUS ORGANISATION	Almost by definition, it is easier for a large organisation to be a respected household name that will impress a future employer and give staff the feeling that they are working for a recognised prestigious organisation. The whole endeavour to create an employer brand that is synchronised with a consumer brand and backed up by corporate social responsibility initiatives is far more the stuff of larger organisations.	Small organisations must concentrate on ensuring that they are respected within their sector even if they are not a household name. Large organisations have greater risk of a rogue division harming the respect with which they are held.

JOB SATISFACTION

ACHIEVEMENT	Smaller organisations have less scope to offer a breadth of ongoing achievement unless they are growing into larger organisations. There are fewer opportunities to turn round an ailing branch or division or set up a new venture. Of course, such opportunities are open to only a small number in larger organisations and so it is vital to identify the correct people to whom you give such incentives. However, small organisations are probably better positioned to be flexible in offering early opportunity for achievement.	All organisations must think creatively about how to create opportunities for people to achieve. Large organisations must mimic the flexibility of small organisations to offer the opportunities to achieve early in people's careers.
RESPECT AND RECOGNITION	So much about offering respect and recognition depends on the individual boss that small organisations probably offer the best and worst whereas larger organisations will tend to average out across managers. It has repeatedly been pointed out that people leave managers rather than organisations and so any sized organisation needs to ensure that its managers are the reason for people staying rather than leaving.	Small organisations cannot afford to have a curmudgeonly owner-manager turning staff off and causing the best to leave.
AUTONOMY	Small organisations have a great opportunity to allow people to function without the restrictions of big company policies. However, it is probably easier for them to	Large organisations have to be imaginative in offering the freedom of a small organisation. For example, during the dot-com boom large organisations tried

	host a micro-manager who will not delegate whereas in a larger company this type of management. style would hopefully be picked up by senior people in the organisation.	to satisfy autonomy needs by sponsoring incubators.
WORK–LIFE BALANCE	There is no particular reason why any sized organisation should be at an advantage. All organisations need to challenge any restrictions on flexibility. However, large organisations are probably more restricted in terms of setting precedents that they would not wish to be taken up by all staff.	
CONGRUENT VALUES	The values of small organisations are perhaps clearer and starker than those of larger organisations. There is therefore more opportunity for people to find themselves in a highly congruent or highly alien environment. Small firms could gain an advantage by offering quite a bold statement of values which will be a strong retainer for those sharing them (e.g., the Body Shop in its early days).	
SENSE OF FUN	There does not seem to be any necessary advantage attached to size. A lot will depend upon the individual manager or leader of the small organisation or unit of the large organisation.	Large organisations must give leaders latitude to build their teams in the way that will appeal to their teams.

Table 3. Large and small organisations' engagement USPs.

The caricature of the large firm is that it is better positioned to offer the package and employability whereas the small organisation might be better positioned to offer job satisfaction. However, as has been seen, the small firm can seek to match its larger competitors for people in terms of the package and by thinking creatively about employability. Likewise, the large organisation can match the small in terms of offering job satisfaction. It will do so by behaving as a portfolio of small organisations, each run by a high quality leader.

Overall, it can be seen that smaller organisations do not necessarily suffer a disadvantage as long as they are successful and can fund the meeting of people's needs. Whether this is the case depends upon the reason for their being small. If they are small because they are not particularly successful, they will be caught in a vicious circle, remaining less successful because they will not be able to attract and retain the best people. If they are small through choice and successful at what they do (the Savile Row tailor) then there is no reason why they cannot trump their larger rivals.

ELICITING NEEDS

How do you know what people's needs are? One way is to empathise and gain an insight into what people might want – and not want – and how they might react. Psychologists are well–placed in this task as their training is to understand people's responses – and to anticipate them. Which is not to say that you

have to employ a psychologist, but at least you have to put a psychologist's hat on. The other way or at least the complement of this empathy is to ask people. Fairly recently, a group of American researchers led by Bagozzi (2003) published a method for uncovering people's motives that is both simple and effective. Essentially you ask people to focus on a current or future job and get them to answer three columns of questions:

- **First**, they are asked to state five reasons for going for the new job / staying with the present one.

- **Second**, for each reason, they are asked to state why that reason is important to them

- **Finally**, they are asked to look at each statement of importance and state why that is important.

Using this methodology, you uncover the underlying motives the person has for being in / choosing a job. You will find that people definitely differ in their reasons and about what is important; however, you will also find that the reasons fit broadly within the triangle of needs.

BRANDING

Just as each individual has his/her own needs, so each organisation has an identity in terms of the needs it is particularly good at satisfying and the way in which it does so. The employment proposition and employer branding describe what an organisation has on offer and reminds us that, although trying to attend to the needs of each individual is important, organisations cannot be all things to all people. They have to be distinct and to some extent they have to be what the people they want are looking for. Of course, there is a circularity here, but the basic argument is that, for example, Foxtons has an identity as an estate agent quite distinct from Savills. Presumably, each firm knows what sort of person they need to be successful. As organisations, Foxtons and Savills then need to live out the personalities that will be attractive to the people they need.

The arenas of winning customers and winning employees have become highly overlapping. The image that the organisation presents to customers is an image that is received by current and potential employees. And the way the organisation treats its staff has an impact on its image with customers. This is illustrated vividly by the concerns of companies not to be seen as amongst those that exploit labour in the third world.

COMMITMENT: A WINNING TACTIC?

Talented people are talented because they can be trusted to deliver – either delivering directly to the customer of the organisation or delivering to the organisation itself – particularly as leaders of customer delivery staff. Trust of course goes both ways and organisations must ensure that those that they trust in turn have trust in their employers. Having attended to people's needs, organisations must offer commitment long-term if they are to expect it in return, Woodruffe, (1999). Other things being equal people will prefer to have their needs met in a relatively secure environment rather than one where there is considerable doubt about the continuity of the employment. Offering commitment does not mean offering a guarantee. It means conveying that leaders are putting prime importance on the organisation's future and that people will not be the first to be jettisoned if the going gets tough. Otherwise, people will be tempted to jump before they are pushed.

In summary:

- You retain people by meeting their needs

- Commitment should be part of the deal you are offering

- Accurate identification of talent is vital

BRINGING IT ALL TOGETHER

ENGAGING AND RETAINING PEOPLE ARE OF SPECIAL IMPORTANCE AND DIFFICULTY AT THE VERY TIME THAT YOU ARE RETRENCHING AND MAKING REDUNDANCIES

Talent management in 2009 faces the extra challenge of having to be done on a shoestring. It also has to be done in the context of uncertainty and the stress that is thereby engendered. Nevertheless, all staff have to be engaged to give their best and the talented élite on whom the future depends have to be retained. Indeed, these imperatives are particularly important in the context of survival.

How well this is done depends a great deal on communication by the leaders of organisations and individual managers. It also depends crucially on their authenticity. People will be disengaged and will leave at the first opportunity if they perceive themselves to be sacrificed readily to preserve their leaders' positions and rewards. To the extent that the meeting of people's needs is being curtailed, (e.g., less reward, less development, fewer prestige projects) such cuts and changes need to be explained carefully and honestly. There needs to be clarity on what is happening and why and what the future holds. Above all, people need to perceive the genuine commitment of employers. This means holding people in respect and showing that everything possible is being done to preserve people's psychological contract and ultimately their employment contract. Otherwise, employers will create a store of cynicism that will be hard to dispel when better times return.

Talent management in 2009 offers a tremendous challenge and the opportunity for those who are good at it to stand out and help their organisations stand out through their people. To make its contribution, talent management has to be strategic. It has to be clear to all in the organisation what the talent manager is trying to achieve and how this is being done. The components of talent management have to be integrated and support each other.

It is at once gloomy and optimistic to say that the recession is bound to identify both those who are gifted at talent management and those who have until now survived by flinging money at the problem. As such it is a most interesting time.

REFERENCES

Bagozzi et al. (2003). Hierarchical representation of motives in goal setting. *Journal of Applied Psychology, 88(5),* 915–943

Cannon, J A and McGee, R. (2007). *Talent management and succession planning.* **CIPD**

Cappelli, P. (2008). Talent management for the twenty–first century. *Harvard Business Review,* March, 74–81

CIPD. (2005). *How to select a coach.* **http://www.cipd.co.uk/coachingatwork/presales/ How+to+select+a+coach.htm**

CIPD. (2007). *Coaching in organisations.* **CIPD**

CIPD. (2008). *Employee turnover and retention factsheet.* **http://www.cipd.co.uk/subjects/hrpract turnover/empturnretent.htm?IsSrchRes=1**

Department of Health. (2004). *The NHS knowledge and skills framework.* **London: Department of Health Publications**

Eyre, E. (2007). Serious games are the road map to success. *Training Journal,* November 2007

Heilman, M E and Okimoto, T G. (2008). Motherhood: A potential source of bias in employment decisions. *Journal of Applied Psychology, 93(1),* 189–198

Hom, P W, Roberson, L and Ellis, A D. (2008). Challenging conventional wisdom about who quits: Revelations from corporate America. *Journal of Applied Psychology,* 2008, *93(1),* 1–34

Howitt, D and Owusu–Bempah, J. (1990). The pragmatics of institutional racism: Beyond words, *Human Relations. 43(9),* 885–899

Kolb, D A. (1984). *Experiential learning: Experience as the source of learning and development.* **New Jersey: Prentice Hall Inc.**

Levashina, J and Campion, M A. (2007). Measuring faking in the employment interview: Development and validation of an interview faking behaviour scale. *Journal of Applied Psychology, 92(6),* 1638–1656

Lim, C, Winter, R and Chan, CCA. (2006). Cross cultural interviewing in the hiring process: Challenges and strategies. *The Career Development Quarterly, 54,* 265–268

Martin, P D and Pope, J. (2008). Competency–based interviewing – has it gone too far? *Industrial and Commercial Training, 40(2),* 81–86

Pyburn, K M Jr, Ployhart, R E and Kravitz, D A. (2008). The diversity–validity dilemma: Overview and legal context. *Personnel Psychology, 61(1),* 143–151

Silvester, J. (2008). Identifying leaders: Ethnicity and perceived leadership potential and work. *Organisational Psychology and Ethnicity Research Seminar,* 8th July 2008

Syedain, Hashi. (2008). Diversified statements. *People Management,* 27 November, 30–33

Woodruffe, C. (1999). *Winning the talent war: A strategic approach to attracting, developing and retaining the best people.* Chichester: John Wiley

Woodruffe, C. (2007). *Development and Assessment Centres: Identifying and developing competence, 4th edition.* London: Human Assets Ltd.

www.ingramcontent.com/pod-product-compliance
Lightning Source LLC
Chambersburg PA
CBHW041450210326
41599CB00004B/198